Ecstasy Will Have to Do

poems by

Aspen Bernath-Plaisted

Finishing Line Press
Georgetown, Kentucky

Ecstasy Will Have to Do

Copyright © 2017 by Aspen Bernath-Plaisted
ISBN 978-1-63534-086-0 First Edition
All rights reserved under International and Pan-American Copyright Conventions.
No part of this book may be reproduced in any manner whatsoever without written permission from the publisher, except in the case of brief quotations embodied in critical articles and reviews.

Publisher: Leah Maines

Editor: Christen Kincaid

Cover Art: Aspen Bernath-Plaisted

Author Photo: Tim Bernath-Plaisted

Cover Design: Elizabeth Maines

Printed in the USA on acid-free paper.
Order online: www.finishinglinepress.com
also available on amazon.com

Author inquiries and mail orders:
Finishing Line Press
P. O. Box 1626
Georgetown, Kentucky 40324
U. S. A.

Table of Contents

Ecstasy Will Have to Do 1
This Dirt Road 2
A Moment Out of Grief 4
That Which Is the Beauty 5
Angel Wings 6
Weaver's Story 7
A Rich Life 9
Giant and Great Blue Spruces Stand Strong in Legacy 10
Deer Have Their Ways 12
We Are a Planet Rejoicing 14
Purple Slippers 16
Life's Eclipse 17
Resurrection Lives in Me 19
I Pray Everyday 20
How Does That Music Know? 21
Reading Rumi 22
Quick Silver 23
Perhaps 25
Holy Water and Spirit of the Wind 26
The Face in the Frame 27
The Cardinal 28
Deer Path 29
Cupid's Arrow 30

In honor and in loving memory of Sylvia and Leonard Bernath

With deepest gratitude for my dear husband, Tim, who continues to support me in all ways every step along the way, and for my beautiful family and friends. We are after all not islands. We are instead community.

ECSTASY WILL HAVE TO DO

I am listening now
to an exquisite quiet
that rings so true
with a vibrancy that cannot be denied
its sacred origin

It is not just the sound
of rustling leaves in autumn trees
now preparing to release
nor is it just
the proclaiming of our feathered friends
urgent in migration
etching zig zags and diagonals
in the graying sky

No, I am listening to something more
it is the spell that happens
when the outer life
arrives and joins in harmony
with my inner peace
melting all distance in time and space
and dissolving all illusions
of a body alone
and separate from
and perhaps without spirit
enhancing its experience

Hard as I try
no word comes to my lips
true enough to convey this listening
so ecstasy will have to do

THIS DIRT ROAD

Ah, this dirt road breathes deep sighs of peace and joy,
quietude and solitude,
and whispers the footsteps of
deer and rabbits and so many brothers and sisters
that scurry about with the pleasure of sweet earth
beneath their hooves and toes.

This dirt road is graced by the shadows of
sandhill cranes gliding, clacking, laughing overhead
red-tailed hawks screeching their presence, and
red-winged blackbirds flitting from tree to tree.

And the creek meanders over, under, across
and sometimes swims the width of road
while cattails stand their ground in swamps and
frogs have won anew arenas,
and this dirt road offers a soft gentle bed for
those little beings awaiting a new day
to emerge once again.

This dirt road emerges again relieved by its
spongy, springy, tender body
that no longer sends dust to sting the eyes
and fill the nostrils of all animals who alight upon it,
but instead now receives the feet with a velvet touch
to cushion and help them along their way.

Listen…this dirt road tells the story of
dogs astray and woodchucks announcing
that spring has arrived this very day;
of horses and humans sharing relationship and companionship
as little children smile upon their backs and
wave to neighbors who lift their heads out of flower beds
to say good day, good day.

And sometimes it holds the memory of the cat
with lovely stripes or colors of black and white
who did not make it home that night,
while the flashlights searching and yearning
illuminated the tears that streaked the faces and the glimmer of hope
that was left with the footsteps now etched
in the memory of this dirt road.

Let us not forget the secrets, sworn never to reveal,
that this dirt road buries deep within its layers
perhaps about the children at last free
to hurry recklessly on wheels making grooves
within this dirt road,
or the friends that wander carefreely
and mingle stories and share their truths,
or the lovers holding hands and speaking dreams
and fears and words not said before
that come out freely and softly between them and
leave a trace of romance that fairies catch
and then shriek in playful ecstasy.

A MOMENT OUT OF GRIEF

Sometimes I can step out of grieving for those who pass
and leave this earth in so many ways
with different faces and premature stages of life
still budding and waiting and desiring growth

At least I think I can
even just for a moment or two
journey with the unraveling thread
that makes the veil just a little thinner
almost enough to grasp
just the beginning edge of a concept
that so subtly allows my lip to curve
just a bit at the corner
to form a smile so quiet
it is truly only recognized and felt within
as being touched by grace

Perhaps angels hold my heart
that in dismay suspends breath
then gently
of course
miraculously
the heart is released

Sometimes I can step out of grieving
and feel the inescapable truth
the transience inherent
in the infinite grains of sand
in the monk's painting
certain only that the rain will come
without vengeance
it will simply come

THAT WHICH IS THE BEAUTY

She wandered around aimlessly amongst the weeping willows
and she was weeping too.
Only you couldn't see the tears.
She wasn't quite invisible, not really.
Her veils were transparent,
but you couldn't see her tears, not really.

But I knew that she wept; I saw it in her form.
A surreal image projected through the mist.
A frail frame bent, looking for what isn't,
and missing that which is.
That which is the beauty of the woman that she is.
She wasn't quite invisible, not really.
Her isolation was translucent
but you couldn't see the tears, not really.

But I knew that she wept; I saw it in her gaze.
A distant glance at nothing,
a frozen glare at pain.
A distant glance at nothing, she said she didn't see.
A frozen glare at pain, she said she didn't feel.

She wasn't quite invisible, not really.
Her face was like a journal disclosing many days.
Many days of wandering
amongst the weeping willows.
She was weeping too, and now I saw the tears.
Rivers joyously cascading
and releasing all her fears.

Many years have come and gone, and she has found her way.
Re-tracing all her footsteps
and what was missed throughout those days.
While looking for what isn't and missing that which is.
That which is the beauty of the woman that she is.

ANGEL WINGS

Love can be like that.
Yes, I remember making angel wings in the snow.
As a child, everything seeming so much bigger than life.
And I never got cold,
warmed by the energy of play and love.

Yes, love can be like that.
I remember my mom calling me into the house
and I walked in all dripping of snow and ice.
Rosy cheeks and frozen toes.
She'd help to undress me,
and I'd sit by the heater warming my feet and drinking hot milk.
Rub my toes, please.

Yes, love can be like that.
Well, making angel wings is probably even more fun
than building a snowman.
A snowman just melts,
but angel wings take flight.
Limitless, they know
no boundaries, just vapors breaking free.

Yes, love can be like that.
Funny thing, they leave their landing mark.
A mere outline of what was once there.
A melted shadow announcing a joyous
commitment to return.
Twinkling fairy lights showing off the sky,
and blessing my life.

Yes, love can be like that.

WEAVER'S STORY

She sat crossed-legged and straight,
her back supported only by habit and resolve.
A shawl loosely folded around her shoulders,
promising relief, born only in faith
that it would provide the necessary warmth and comfort
throughout the cool fall evening.

Her face was still.
Wrinkles winding pathways around its surface.
Some lines were new and light,
barely claiming residence to the spot they occupied.
Others were deep and grooved, carved into permanence
by a sculptor's harsh hand and a relentless sun.
Still others were worn and faded,
indifferent to the story that once marked their birth.
Now scrubbed and erased,
no longer a scar, yet the memory remains.

Her hands were strong and patient.
Slowly and precisely guiding the layers of dried grass and vine.
The light, now dim as the sun lowered in the sky, did not
disturb her rhythm.
Fingers once timid and unsure,
now easily sensed their direction
and gracefully laced the twine,
row after row, around the universe that was hers.

Her eyes were not vacant; they were deep.
Her stillness hid the symphony with which her prayers danced.
It was never the same:
sometimes a monotone low and intense,
sometimes a climax of discovery and decision,
often a lullaby secure and reassuring
offering communication of love and tenderness.

She followed the path of the sunset and slowly stopped her work.
Her eyes caught the colors that painted the sky,
as she silently blessed the mother and caressed the earth.

A RICH LIFE

Did you think that life would be
a piece of cake
rich…luscious…smooth
chocolate fudge cake
just waiting to ease
and caress and sweetly sterilize
or disenfranchise
this rich thick expanding
and contracting life
by erasing countless views of reality
conflicting and confusing explosions of inconsistencies
convoluted and refusing to be pureed?

I myself would suggest
a slice of strawberry rhubarb pie
in which the tongue welcomes
the stringent stalks
of beautiful maroon
delightfully adorned with strawberry juices
not too saucy
as to make one forget the rhubarb in life
but urges one to celebrate and savor
the sugar and spice illustrations
of a rich life
for they are what we learn to cherish
in a most remarkable way.

GIANT AND GREAT BLUE SPRUCES STAND STRONG IN LEGACY

You left so much
In the quaking wake following
The discontinuance of the breath
You chose to dismiss
In one quick heart breaking explosion
The bullet took the path of least resistance
Through the sweetest
And most innocent chamber
Never expecting to be put to rest,
Relieved of all duties,
And released of all that was too much to pacify

And so you left
With sprinkles of insights and wisdom
Memories and sentiments yearning to be understood
All scratched and sometimes crossed out
Upon fragments of paper – even napkins –
All left to fend for themselves
And to play hide and seek with us,
The finders of such jewels,
Now spattered and tattered with tears
And witnessed for all they were worth
The full worth of understanding a man's heart
Made too soft and sensitive to survive

There are blue spruces
That live on this land
They share with us
And we call it home
Held within these spruces and so many more
Lives the pictures of a man's tenderness
In planting a seedling with love
That some save for a baby
Or soft cuddly puppy…
Gentle gentle images

Of placing the roots in the ground
And caressing with soil and water
With canvas secured to protect from the wind and the cold
And barriers to deter the deer

Today giant and great blue spruces
Stand strong in legacy

DEER HAVE THEIR WAYS

deer sneak up the hill
behind the blue green house
that treasures itself in worth
with adornments of flowers
and vegetable gardens
now safely fortified
within fences old and wired and lopsided
and those freshly cut from wood
made noble and strong
fit to secure the livelihood
of poppies and peonies
daylilies and elegant iris queens
tulips and roses alike
all such treats for the sweet sweet deer
who have their ways

they tiptoe up and approach
closer and closer
with nose to the ground
munching grass along the way
and finally come to a halt
standing before the great guard
they conclude it is not wise
to use the energy
that must be conserved for other purposes
and so choose not to leap
but instead
accept the sacrificed mums
left out before them
it is a joy to see the deer standing there
doing what they do

we shall not fight the ways of the deer
who run for their lives with bushy white tail
standing high in alert

during the hunting season
that comes about like clockwork
that they have grown to understand
we shall pray for them

WE ARE A PLANET REJOICING

We are a people
a nation
a planet
We came as one from oneness
unique and in common.

When did it happen;
when did we fall from one
and become many divided in status
and driven by boundaries?
Split not in yin/yang harmony and balance
as complements reflecting wholeness.
Not as a child seeking mother
or feminine seeking masculine
or up seeking down.
When did it happen
that the yin/yang became frozen in division,
in ugliness, and in greed?
Or, in the face that could not reach out
beyond the fear of scarcity?

I have pondered this long and hard
since being a young girl
with stars in the eyes
that remembered wholeness
with rays that traveled beyond separation
with a zip code too big to commit to memory.
It is not hard to recall the faces of hatred
mocking an existence and denying membership
to love and the have enough club.
There is no permanence.
Even the permafrost in Siberia
must give way to new structures, new concepts
for securing comfort and peace on the planet.

Today we are a people
a nation striving
transforming and releasing the false permanence
of old and tarnished ways.
Rejecting those heavy burdens
that were so hard to carry
and kept us empty within our islands.
Now surrendering to the joy
that awaits us in new thought
and rich in the fullness of new moments,
we are a planet rejoicing.

PURPLE SLIPPERS

I walked into the store today
it was so easy
and I bought a pair of purple slippers
oh how I love purple
and the soft lofty inside
is quite a cushion for my feet

then I remembered
how soft and cushioned my life was
is
always has been
yes
I have had heartaches
and loss
that is true
but I've always had loving arms
to fall deeply into
to receive a safe sweet haven
from tragedy and pain
and
a home to let go in
with a meal
that quiets the panic of emptiness

I walked into the store today
just marched right in
there was nothing keeping me
from those purple slippers
and when I left
I still had dollars in my wallet
the woman ringing the bell
held the door open
wide enough for me to exit
and she wished me a good day

LIFE'S ECLIPSE

Shadows fall and cloud the joy in my heart.
There is stillness as a separation ensues
insidiously polarizing heart and mind.
A vast desert grows.

Thoughts, feelings all dance by.
I can almost touch them... almost
yet the distance is so exaggerated
and the path is foggy.

Do I have cotton in my eyes
and bricks in my head?
Heavy... I feel so heavy and so very tired.
I want to float and wrestle with this sorrow tomorrow.
There's always tomorrow.

Even the moon's eclipse is brief.
Behind the shadow there is light;
the curtain is drawn and
instructions are given.
The darkness is lifted
revealing a rebirth of illumination
as a statement of faith
illustrating the spiritual continuity
of nature's way.

A child's life quickly drains
as life's eclipse cast shadows
across her face.
Youth subsides and ageless
wondering eyes stare back at me.
Wisdom catches up and condenses
a life span of experience
into single moments.

Soon there will be no pain
for even the moon's eclipse is brief.
Thankfully behind the shadow there is light.
The curtain is drawn and
instructions are given.
The darkness is lifted
revealing a rebirth of illumination
as a statement of faith
illustrating the spiritual continuity
of nature's way.

RESURRECTION LIVES IN ME

It is hard to gleefully embrace the bitter cold in winter
when one has grown so weary
and expects so very much
while refusing to behold the lovely mural
of winter bringing spring
without which spring simply could not hold or bring
the power and the gifts that it truly is to me.

Found in thawing opaque waters
slowly plotting to break through
bearing witness for all to see the wonders
as the blue sky sunny presence
spreads its warmth and brilliant hue
giving glimpses rare and deep below
in places where the seekers seek
but somehow seldom know.

It is hard to match the beauty of this captivating time
with crocus peaking through the ice
and trying to survive the nibble
of the rabbits frantically waiting for this time
with sparkling ice diamonds
profoundly glittering amongst
the tops of trees
inviting resurrection
as ultimately
resurrection lives in me.

I PRAY EVERY DAY

I pray every day
Sometimes with tears
Over years, many years
Please help me know you
the big You, the all You
the everything, loving, divine, and sublime you.

I pray in the way
That I hope
Helps me find you
With candles and music
And ways that enshrine You

The You that is part me
And lives deep inside me
The You that defines me
And never defiles me
The You that is larger than life
In all ways
The You that finds peace
Hidden deep within strife
With a well that is flowing and
Honors all life

HOW DOES THAT MUSIC KNOW?

How does that music know
how to weave its way into my soul
setting free that which I may not
have met before?

Turning the color inside this room
to twilight sunset rose
maybe it is a new chamber
or no, just ancient and unknown
only to be opened by the key
that angels sing

How does that music know
what language it must speak for
inducing magic tonals
and eliciting the opening
of the great secret vault?

The opera singer vibrates
until there is a glass explosion
like wrinkles in time
frequencies that must collide

Monks chant synchronized and soulful
sounding until the inner and outer
universes find each other to be in
harmonic agreement
It is the mysterious way

READING RUMI

I was reading Rumi last night
Each sentence
A well so deep

It is necessary to dwell
And let it seep
Freely and quietly through me

Through my mind's eye
Through my heart's center
Ready to receive the awakening

That shifts the power of command
To my spirit
Who already knows the ways

Of infinite love, compassion, forgiveness,
And in this wisdom
I too am free

QUICK SILVER

thank-you thank-you thank-you
from the bottom of my sometimes
tired heart
i want to scream for joy
when the words come
they come out just like
quick silver

slipping into consciousness
this pen in hand
comes alive
with ink mirroring the stream
of flowing pleasure
as letter characters are freed
by the calligrapher's stroke

just as steam escapes
and releases out of engines
the pressure relaxes
and does not continue
to build up

there is pressure accrued
when living life
on earth
the pressure of
hearing things
and seeing things
of knowing things and feeling things
the pressure of being a human being

all human beings are responsible
for so much welfare
or lacking thereof
the way of a pure and true human being

can be a pressure but
the joyous release comes
from experiencing and feeling
a true connection to a way
of honoring all the miracles of life
it is the way of deep love

PERHAPS

There always seems to be
Two sides of a story
The other side of the coin
And of course, on the other hand…

When playing ping pong
That ball of love and hate
Pain and elation
Jealousy and joy
Appears to bounce randomly
With no will of its own

Up and down the roller coaster
Seemingly just a pawn
In the scheme of things
Disconnected, far removed
Insignificant acts
Or so we like to think…

But consider if you will
The will, no pun intended
Perhaps the way of the will
Is clearer than one thinks
And senses the truth
In all directions of the road
Sometimes less traveled
For fear of standing out
Or even being vulnerable

Perhaps the Little Prince understood
That his glorious rose was the
Only side of the story

HOLY WATER AND SPIRIT OF THE WIND

I am not offended by the April rains
nor by grandmother wind's announcement
that it is time for her to carry away
and disperse old energies

I say bravo
please come and do as you may
for there is much work
to be done

Please cleanse for renewal
for these are changing times
and true to the spirit of the wind
it is indeed time

Time to take a long strong breath
then sigh in gratitude and release
I do remember hearing once in a ceremonial dream
"it is time to release that which is meant to be released
and to receive that which is meant to be received"

I say Amen to this
the fresh rainwater understands this language
for it speaks to it innately
about that which it already knows
to be the truth of its purpose
and understands this gift

So send down if you will
your tiny droplets of hope
as you promise to renew
 and nourish all those in need
now add your crystal sparkle
to preserve onto this earth
that which is dearly holy

THE FACE IN THE FRAME

I noticed the young man's face in the frame on the wall
He looked like such a child – yes
He was a man child
Looking so out of place
In the lofty marine uniform

The attire fit
His hat sat just right on his head
And the jacket looked
To have visited a tailor
It was clearly his suit of choice

He enlisted you know
On impulse
It was plainly the thing for him to do
That face – so naïve
Was taken by impulse

The eyes in the photo
Were forced to view
That which was surely
Beyond imagination
Of all young men

Really a child
Now recruited by a world
That some would call
Committed to protecting its youth

When he comes home
I wonder where he will hide
What his eyes have seen

THE CARDINAL

I am grateful for the cardinal that sits upon the dead tree branches.
The highest point is where he can be seen,
delicately balanced and singing a persistent melody.

Naked tree branches extend out toward the sun.
A chilling wind has made them frail and brittle appendages
no longer serving for the continuance of life.

Now a tree no longer capable of nourishing its own splintered structure,
yet a cardinal sits upon the dead tree branches,
and glows red against the sun's amber rays.

There is dignity after death.

DEER PATH

my feet follow the path freshly left by the deer
over curves and between the evergreen pines
some embarrassed to display the cold crystal white
that has covered their girth with this sparkling sight
while others like skeletons
telling stories of struggles not won
with the wind and the storms well back into time

my feet follow the path freshly left by the deer
as my eyes gently veer to the tops of tree branches
commingled with a sky showing winter and blue
with the sun looking cold
while still shining through
as the snow frosting covers the low slanting roof
knowing most surely
it will soon join
the soft covered earth

the deer keep on hoofing
i could never keep up
making hoops and large rings
and diagonals touching all corners of things
to places where feet simply choose not to go
the deer own this earth now covered in snow

CUPID'S ARROW

Cupid's arrow is so revered
What lover of love
Does not stand in line
Waiting
Just to be so thoroughly struck
So the world really
Can stand still
Because
Sometimes
It actually takes time
To notice
What may have been
Right before one's eyes
Though much to busy to see
What so many others
Already have noticed
The subtleties of love
The most beautiful of all ways
Do not always seem to merit
In and of themselves
The recognition they deserve
And so
Instead
That mighty arrow of cupid's arrives
Slyly…on the fly
It knows the way to catch one
Even in transit and suddenly
A deep surprise alights.

Ecstasy Will Have to Do is Aspen Bernath-Plaisted's third publication. Over a period of five years her poems and short essays have made frequent appearances in community newspaper, *The Nexus News*, of Lansing MI, for which she also hosted a holistic self-help column with several other panel members.

Aspen teaches classes in: Poetic Expressions, The Relationship Between Spirituality, Self-Esteem and Empowerment, Intentional Well Being, Qigong, as well as several topics involving increased awareness for positive change. She has been a Hypnotherapist and Social Worker for 36 years and a Qigong Instructor for 18 years. Clear and heartfelt communications remain a major theme in all that she does.

Aspen continues to live in her country home with her husband where they have cultivated gardens for 30 years. Her love for the earth, and all varieties of inhabitants, has been a large source of her writing inspirations.

www.ingramcontent.com/pod-product-compliance
Lightning Source LLC
LaVergne TN
LVHW041506070426
835507LV00012B/1365